Unlocking
the Supernatural
Realm Through Prayer

Elizabeth Dankaro

Grosvenor House
Publishing Limited

This book is published by
Grosvenor House Publishing Ltd
Link House
140 The Broadway, Tolworth, Surrey, KT6 7HT.
www.grosvenorhousepublishing.co.uk

A CIP record for this book
is available from the British Library

ISBN 978-1-83975-986-4

Dedication

I dedicate this book to the Lord Jesus Christ. When I was lost, confused and miserable, not knowing what to do, He came into my life and gave me hope to live again.

I also want to dedicate this book to my late sister Mrs Nancy S. Torsabo, whom the Lord used to mentor me and taught me on how to pray with scriptures in the Bible. And to also listen to the Holy Spirit to speak back to me. It is my prayer that as many that read this book, their prayer life will never remain the same.

Acknowledgments

I want to thank everyone who has encouraged me, assisted me and prayed for me during the process of writing this book. Especially my children (twins) Joshua and Caleb, their wives, my grandchildren and all members of my family. My special thanks to Precious Da Costa, sister to Braulia (my daughter in law) who not only supported me in prayer, but paid fully for the book to be published. Thank you Grosvenor House Publishing and Staff for the wonderful job editing this book and support of this work. My appreciation also goes to my Pastor Gabriel Ikyemtu and his wife and the members of Victory Life Bible Church London for their support and care.

Unlocking Supernatural Realm through Prayer

Why don't answers to our prayers always come? What hindrances prevent the prayer power of God from flowing in believers' lives and producing answers?

In this book, the author reveals secrets from the scriptures that unlock the blessing of divine encounter with the Lord through prayer. The author begins by taking a look at common misconceptions that block our divine encounter in prayer. She then cites cases where many Christians proclaim that they have prayed, but never hear from God. Many lived in frustration and kept wandering or even questioned whether God hear prayers. When doubts creep into their lives, that can open the door to the devil. By removing hindrances to answers via the principles outlined in this book, believers will hold the key to divine encounter with Lord

About the Author

A prayerful person is a person who chooses to fight personal and spiritual battles through prayer and the wisdom of the Lord, instead of their own strength, Elizabeth Dankaro has been known for about three decades today to be a woman of prayer. She is blessed with twins Joshua and Caleb. They are also married and blessed with children. Elizabeth's daughters-in-law are Jayde and Braulia. Her grandchildren are Niyah, Amari, Elleora and Raiyah.

Chapter one

WALKING WITH GOD

In the book of Genesis 5:22-24, the Bible records: 'And Enoch walked with God after he begat Methuselah three hundred years, and begat sons and daughters. And all the days of Enoch were three hundred sixty and five years, and Enoch walked with God: and he was not; for God took him.'

The above scripture states that Enoch walked with God. In other words, he had a deep relationship or deep intimacy with God. God knew Enoch and Enoch, in turn, knew God, and would talk to Him face to face. Even though Enoch was a family man (husband and father), he walked with God, and at the end, we are told from the above scripture, God took him. Enoch did not die, but was translated alive into God's kingdom. Enoch, during his lifetime on earth, practised what we call waiting on God.

WAITING ON GOD

The first time I heard about waiting on God, it was after prayer time, with Pastor Andy Eze of Peculiar People Ministries, here in London, UK. It took several months to grasp what he was saying, however, I began to search the Biblical Scripture and make an inquiry from the Lord. Suddenly, the light came, and the scales from my spiritual eyes fell off. Waiting on God means having a close fellowship with God. In other words, being in constant touch with God, developing and maintaining intimate knowledge with the Lord on a continuous basis, continuous habitation with God, being in his presence.

God desires all his children to have intimacy with Him. As a Father, he wants us to know Him, visit Him in his kingdom. Just like we know and have fellowship with our earthly parents, the Lord, our God, want us, through the blood of Jesus, to come boldly to his throne of mercy and have fellowship with Him. God desires to have fellowship with us, so also is the devil.

Satan also tries to appear as the Angel of Light (2 Corinthians 11:14). In fact, he may even try to look like our Lord Jesus; however, a closer look at the devil reveals that he has not got the nail prints or marks, nor the wounds on his hands or feet. Sometimes, when my spiritual eyes are opened and I see someone appearing to me as my Lord Jesus, and I am not sure, when I rebuke such appearance in Jesus's name, immediately I see the person vanish in a hurry. It is important, as a believer in the Lord Jesus, not to chase for visions without his word. Our vision must be backed up with his word, and we must also spend time studying his word.

For many of us Christians who are praying and listening for Him to speak back to us, there is no problem. But when it comes to praying and waiting not only to hear the Lord speak, but to see Him face to face, there can be a problem. Our mindset, or man-made tradition, states that it is impossible to see God, for we are sinners. I have heard testimonies from people who are not Christians saying that if Jesus is real, they want to see Him. Jesus always answered their prayers, thus leading them to become strong believers in Him.

When I became born again in the 1980s, I used to have visions, and sometimes, in my dreams, I would see myself caught up in heaven. I remember, one time, standing before this loving being, at the throne of God, and just admiring his beauty and power and strength. He took me and put me on his lap, covered me with his wings (Ps 91). When I woke up, I was not happy to find myself still in my bed, for in his habitation, I experienced peace and joy.

In 1988, I was travelling from Kaduna to Ilorin in Nigeria by plane for an official conference. I was fasting and praying that day. I had just made myself comfortable in my seat when suddenly my body left me. I saw myself standing before the Lord Jesus, who was on the other side of a beautiful garden; beautiful trees and flowers that I have not seen in this world. The Lord bid me come over, but I couldn't, because there was a big gulf between us. It was deep and dark inside. I made several attempts to cross over, but was afraid, lest I fall inside. The Lord Jesus told me to look at his face, and he stretched forth his hand and took mine. Immediately I was walking in the garden with Him. I was clothed in a garment I cannot describe. There I was with Him; playing and talking with the Lord. While I was in this vision, I suddenly heard the announcement that we would be landing soon. I came back to my natural senses and found myself still sitting on the plane. I was mad again to have come back to this world.

We human beings want God to walk in our ways, but his ways are different from ours. For instance, in this world, we have about maybe eight colours, but colours in heaven are different.

In 1 Corinthians 2:6-9 it says, 'Howbeit we speak wisdom among them that are perfect; yet not the wisdom of this world, nor of the princes of this world, that come to nought: But we speak the wisdom of God in a mystery, even the hidden wisdom, which God ordained before the world unto our glory: Which none of the princes of this world knew, for had they known it, they would not have crucified the Lord of glory. But as it is written, eye hath not seen, nor ear heard; neither have entered into the heart of man the things which God hath prepared for them that love Him.'

Our eyes have not seen what God has kept and reserved for his children. We need to come out of the box and step into the realm of heaven. Many of us have had a real encounter with the Lord, but we have kept this to ourselves, because the Body of Christ is yet to come in terms with heavenly realm programmes, because many of us don't know. We try to shut down those encounters, for they are beyond what we know.

In John 21:25, it is written, 'And there are also many other things which Jesus did, the which, if they should be written every one, I suppose that even the world itself could not contain the books that should be written. Amen.'

There are books in the Bible which are sufficient to maintain our salvation; however, when reading the word of God, we need to keep an open heart. For instance, in one verse, the Holy Spirit may give us several deeper revelations.

Revelations 22:17 says, 'And the spirit and the bride say, Come. And let him that heareth say, Come. And let him that is athirst come. And whosoever will let him take the water of life freely.' This is an open invitation for how far you hunger and thirst for his fellowship with you.

James 4:8 encourages us to draw nigh to God, and he will draw nigh to us. Cleanse your hands, ye sinners; and purify your hearts, ye double minded.

Waiting on God is not easy as it sounds. We need to cleanse our hands, repent of any sin that we commit, purify our hearts and trust in Him. Don't bring self pity prayers to Him, for self pity prayer is also an act of unbelief. God, as our Father, desires to give us the best, as stated in Luke 11:13: 'If ye then, being evil know how to give good gifts unto your children: how much more shall your heavenly Father give the Holy Spirit to them that ask Him?' The best is reserved for us in his kingdom, and God wants these to manifest in our lives. Let us go for them.

In Genesis 3:8, it says, 'And they heard the voice of the Lord God walking in the garden in the cool of the day:

and Adam and his wife hid themselves from the presence of the Lord God amongst the trees of the garden.' Before Adam and Eve fell into sin, the Lord God would come in the cool of the day to talk with them. Adam knew the voice of God and God knew Him. The only teacher that Adam and Eve had at the creation was God Himself. God spoke one language with Adam; a language that was pure, from heaven. God's language. God taught Adam all things about his creation. Things in heaven, earth; the secret of God's creation was not hidden from Adam. Adam and Eve lived both in the visible and invisible world at the same time. Because Adam was taught of God, he (Adam) named all things.

When Jesus, the Son of the living God, came 2000 years ago, he restored that fellowship with our Father in heaven. Through the blood of Jesus and power in his name, those who believe in Jesus have access to his kingdom. More than ever before, God desires to talk to mankind again. The only way to draw near to Him is to talk to God. Many of us rush in prayer without waiting on God to talk back to us and reveal Himself to us. We put on a mask in our prayers.

HOW TO DEVELOP AND WAIT ON GOD

- Build a fellowship with God on a continuous basis; having communion with God daily. Don't hide anything from Him, but talk everything over with Him. Do not hide your emotions from Him. God sees everything hidden in you.
- Practise the art of meditating on his word. Don't just read the Bible to acquire head knowledge.

Let his word gain entrance into your inner being — your heart.
- Wait on God. (Keep silent before Him.)
- Live a life of holiness.
- Be obedient to God and people that rule over you.

When we, as believers, begin to wait on Him, God is pleased to reveal to us the blueprint of our purpose here on earth. Because many of us have no clue about our uniqueness in knowing Him, we tend to copy one another. If someone is excelling in the business or ministry he is called to do, we want to copy. Don't copy methods, but use his principle and come out with your own. Be who you are in Christ Jesus.

Matthew 14:23 says, 'When he had sent the multitudes away, he went up into a mountain apart to pray; and when the evening came, he was there alone.' And Luke 6:12 says, 'And it came to pass in those days, that he went out into the mountain to pray, and continued all night in prayer to God.' If Jesus did this while here on earth, we need to follow in his footsteps. I am not suggesting that you spend all night in prayer, but rather talk to the Lord about it. I have heard testimonies of people who, because of their continuous fellowship with God, do not take the time for them to have a breakthrough in prayers. I have heard people saying that, within fifteen minutes of praying and waiting on the Lord, they have encountered Him.

The Bible says, by strength shall no man prevail. (1Sam. 2:9). This is where the Holy Spirit comes in. We need the Holy Spirit to help us pray according to God's will for us. The Holy Spirit help us in our needs, our infirmities (weaknesses). Most of the time, we don't know what we should pray for, but he, the Holy Spirit, helps us to pray right (Romans 8:26). When we pray in the Holy Ghost language, we break through easily in the spirit, thus aiding us to sit silently and wait for the Lord to speak and show us things we do not know. Jeremiah 33:3 says, 'Call unto me, and I will answer thee, and shew thee great and mighty things, which thou knowest not.'

The Bible declares that our Lord Jesus, when here on earth, did nothing of Himself, but what he sees God the Father does, that he also do likewise (John 5:19). Jesus would get up in the morning, rising up a great while before the day, and would depart into a solitary place to talk to his Father in heaven. (Mark 1:35).

As Christians, if you want a stress-free day and to walk in liberty and peace, set time in the morning to meet with the Lord. Talk about everything with Him, and after talking to Him, don't be in a hurry to rush out. Spend some time before Him in silence, to receive your blueprint from heaven. God desires to talk and reveal Himself to us more than anything else. He is our Father and loves us.

In 1John 1:3, the Bible says, "That which we have seen and heard declare we unto you, that ye also may have fellowship with us: and truly our fellowship is with the Father, and with his Son Jesus Christ."

When we pray and wait on the Lord, the grace of the Lord Jesus Christ, the love of God, and the communion (union) of the Holy Spirit is with us (2Corinthians 13:14).

THREE LEVELS OF IMPARTATION

When we pray and wait on the Lord, we receive levels of impartations:

- From the Father

  In the book of Exodus, when God descended upon Mount Sinai, there was lightning, thundering, loud sounds that no man or beast could breakthrough into to the Lord and gazed at Him. (Exodus 19:18)

  Amos 3:18 says, 'The lion hath roared, who will not fear? The Lord God hath spoken, who can but prophesy?'

  When God the Father speaks, there is a kind of thundering voice that goes into your spirit, driving away fear and breaking chains in your life.

  For a few days I had this experience after praying and waiting silently in his presence: I saw a group of worshippers singing and prophesying over me, I heard a voice thundering, with great lightning that speared through me and brought me to my knees. I noticed a lady beside me who helped me up and began to tell me what the voice was saying. Power and strength were imparted into my soul, producing boldness within me to face the challenges of the day without fear.

- The Lord Jesus Christ.

  The book of Acts 23:11 says, 'And the night following the Lord stood by Him and said, be of good cheer, Paul; for as thou hast testified of me in Jerusalem, so must thou bear witness also at Rome.'

  Also, Revelations 1:10-11 says, 'I was in the spirit on the Lord's day, and heard behind me a great voice as a trumpet, saying, I am Alpha and Omega, the first and the last...' Most times, when the Lord Jesus speaks to me, the impartation I receive in my spirit is so melodious, it is like the moving of water, or the clear and gentle voice of a very good friend.

- The Holy Spirit

  Acts 1:2 says, 'Until the day in which he was taken up, after that he through the Holy Ghost had given commandments unto the apostles whom he had chosen.' The book of 1Kings 19:12 says, 'And after the earthquake a fire, but the Lord was not in the fire and after the fire a still small voice.' The Holy Spirit speaks to us in a gentle and still voice. By that still voice, one receives an impartation of a voice deep in their spirit. You know what to do at any given moment, because he has spoken.

- Heavenly language

    There is only one language in heaven, and that language is love and truth; from the time of Adam, up to the building of the famous tower of Babel, which was not completed. The Bible records that the whole earth was one language and one speech (Genesis 11:1-9). Because of this one language, mankind was determined to build a city and a tower whose top may reach unto heaven. When the Lord came to see the city and the tower, which the children of men built, he confounded their language that they may not understand one another's speech.

    The Lord, therefore, scattered them upon all the faces of the earth, and they left to build the city. This is the reason why we speak different languages today. However, on the day of Pentecost, when believers came together to wait for the promise, as commanded by the Lord Jesus, before ascending to heaven, we are told that they gathered together all with one accord.

    There appeared unto them cloven tongues, like fire, which sat upon each of them. They were filled with the Holy Ghost, and the Spirit gave them utterance. On that day the language that mankind lost at the building of a city and tower of Babel was restored (Acts 2). The heavenly language was restored to mankind when the apostles were filled with Holy Spirit, and they began to speak with other tongues.

In Isaiah 28:11, the Bible says, 'For with stammering lips and another tongue will he speak to his people.' When we speak in unknown tongues (speaking in tongues), the Holy Spirit filters the heavenly language to us as we speak to God the Father, Son, and the Holy Spirit. As God speaks back to us in his heavenly language, the Holy Spirit translates to us in our known language (see 1Cor 12:1-10).

- Have continuous fellowship with the Lord

  Habakkuk 2:1: 'I will stand upon my watch and set me upon the tower, and will watch to see what he will say unto me and what I shall answer when I am reproved.'

  Just like Habakkuk, when we tarry before Him, it is possible to hear his voice, see Him (our Lord Jesus) or even translate into the heavenly realm or spiritual world that is more real than the physical. In preparation to wait on God, it is expected to do the following:

  1. We need to feast on his word. As our physical bodies need food to survive, so do we need the word of God to feed our spiritual being. Become one with Him through the word, and then he will manifest Himself to you. (John 14:21-23).

  2. Live a life of prayer (Luke 18:1).

  3. Amos 3:3: 'Can two walk together except they be agreed?' We need to agree with God's standard. 'God's hand is not shortened, hat he

cannot save; Nor his ear is not heavy, That it cannot hear' (Isaiah 59:1).

We may fast and pray to Him to save us; if there is an unrepented sin, he will hide his face from us. Mathew 5:8 says, 'Blessed are the pure in heart; for they shall see God.' Like Abraham, we need to walk before God and be perfect.

4. Be blameless and live in peace with all men (2Peter 3:14).

5. Live a holy life for our God is holy (1Peter 1:16).

6. In John 6:38, Jesus speaking: 'For I came down from heaven, not to do mine will, but the will of Him that sent me.' Be obedient to the Lord and those that rule over you in this world. You don't pick and choose when it comes to walking with God. Always let his will be done in your life (Matthew 6:10). None of us can choose which family or colour to be born into.

7. Remember, God has his government, and there are protocols that must be maintained. We have no right to suggest to God how he should talk to us.

Sometimes, after praying and waiting silently, I will hear or see nothing. Other times, when I am not expecting Him to show me something, that is when I will have an encounter with the Lord.

On October 15, 2012, I lost my dear sister, Nancy, to cancer. She went to be with the Lord. I was so deeply wounded that I could not even cry. Each time I knelt down to pray, I would say words such as, 'Holy Spirit, stretch out your hands and dry the tears within me.' For six months I was in this condition. Then one day, as I went to sleep, I was transported into another realm. I saw my sister getting ready to meet with God the Father, and the Lord Jesus. I also saw the angels. While talking to Nancy, I saw how fresh and young she looked; very happy, and beaming with a beauty I could not explain. She told me one thing that stuck with me. She said that once you leave the earth, you must follow the protocol of heaven, and that it was time for her to meet the Father. We discussed many things for some time, and when I opened my eyes, I found myself in my room.

When we have fellowship with God on a continuous basis as an intercessor, living in two worlds at the same time is no big deal. Most times I talk to God, and he will show within a split second. He will show me what is going on in a spirit realm at the same time as the physical realm.

In Exodus 33:9-11, Moses spoke to God face to face as one would speak to a friend.

Abraham also called God his friend. When God was going to destroy Sodom and Gomorrah, the Lord appeared to Abraham and showed him what he was going to do to the two cities (Genesis 18:17). Abraham interceded, and his nephew, Lot, and his family escaped. When we pray and wait before the Lord, most of the time He will reveal to us things that can happen to us, our family, community or country. The purpose is to stop Satan from doing evil.

John 15:15: 'Henceforth I call you not servants; for the servant knoweth not what his Lord doeth, but I have called you friends; for all things that I have heard of my Father I have made known unto you.'

The Lord desires to share secrets with us about his creation and teach us to intercede for the souls of men, cities, and families. There are many things in his creation that God wants to show us. Scientists, for many years, have been studying God's creation, which is why billions of dollars are spent researching not only planet earth, but the other planets, which also have beings and spirits. For instance, the cherubim, the 24 elders in the book of Revelation and powerful angelic beings, live on these planets (Ezekiel 1:1, Revelation 4).

Daniel, in the book of Daniel, chapters 7 and 12, had visions of the rise and fall of kingdoms and gave end time prophecies. John, while he was in exile on the island of Patmos, wrote the Book of Revelation. He was caught in heaven, and describes the period between Christ's ascension and His second coming as a time of judgement on earth. He also describes the future of the millennium, the battle of God and Magog, the great white throne judgement, the lake of fire and the new heaven and the new earth.

In Genesis 5:22, we are informed that Enoch walked with God. Also, Jude 1:1-15 says, 'And Enoch also, the seventh from Adam, prophesied of these sayings, behold, the

Lord cometh with ten thousands of his saints, to execute judgement upon all and to convince all that are ungodly among them of all their ungodly deeds which they have ungodly committed, and of their hard speeches which ungodly sinners have spoken against Him.'

Enoch's account is only recorded in Genesis and Jude. However, in the book of Enoch, God revealed to Enoch that He was going to destroy the earth through a flood. Enoch interceded for the earth, and God heard him.

A man called Noah found grace in the eyes of the Lord (see Genesis 6). God saved man and other animals from the flood through Noah and his families. In this end time, God is looking for the man, woman, girl or boy who will have fellowship with Him and intercede for his creation.

Chapter two

Waiting on God

Isaiah 40:31: 'But they that wait on the Lord shall renew their strength; they shall mount up with wings as eagles; they shall run and not be weary, and they shall walk and not faint.'

The early church practised a lot of praying, studying the word, and waiting silently in his presence. In Acts 6, there was murmuring of Grecians against the Hebrews because their widows were neglected in the daily ministration. The disciples were not ready to leave the word of God and serve tables. Rather, they suggested the brethren should appoint men among them to do the business, but they continued to give themselves to prayer and the ministry of the word. The early church realized that the key to enter into the bosom of God was through waiting.

The present church emphasizes more on gifts of the Spirit (Corinthians 12:7-10). However, we read in Mathew 7:21-23, that not everyone that says Lord, shall enter into the kingdom of heaven; only those that do the will of God the Father in heaven. Not even those that prophesied in His name, cast out devils and do much wonderful work in Jesus's name. Members of the

Church must have personal relationships with the Lord and put their trust in the word of God.

Moving in the gifts of the spirit without the fruit of the spirit which is love, joy, peace, longsuffering, gentleness, goodness, faith, meekness, temperance may not allow us into his presence (Galatians 5:22-23).

God confirmed his word with signs and wonders (Mark 16:20). However, the fruits of the spirit manifesting in one's life makes us stand before God. In 1Corinthians 13:1: 'Though I speak with the tongues of men and angels, and have not charity (love), I become as sounding brass or a tinkling cymbal.'

God is a spirit, and anyone that worships Him must worship Him in spirit and truth (John 4:24). God is invisible to the human eye. He is also love, and love is heavenly language. Without compassion in our hearts, we can't do anything. Waiting on Him without having compassion in our hearts will not gift us with presence. I pray that the Lord will fill us with the spirit of compassion; the kind of compassion that moved Jesus when he came to the city of Nain and raised the only son of a widow from the dead.

Luke 7:12-15: "Now when he came nigh to the gate of the city, behold, there was a dead man carried out, the only son of his mother, and she was a widow, and much people of the city was with her. And when the Lord saw her, he had compassion on her, and said unto her, Weep not. And he came and touched the bier, and they that bare Him stood still, and he said, young man, I say unto thee; arise. And he that was dead sat up and began to speak. And he delivered him to his mother.'

To walk in signs and wonders, we must have compassion in our heart and wait on the Lord to show us what to do. With our abilities, we can't do anything.

In Isaiah 40:31: 'But they that wait upon the Lord shall renew their strength; they shall mount up with wings like eagles, they shall run and will not be weary, and they shall walk and not faint.'

The time comes in one's life when serving the Lord becomes burdensome, especially when you are called into the office of intercession. You pray so much that it seems as though your strength is being sapped, and you become weary, or burnt out. Often this happens to us when all we know is to pray to God, but we will not create time to wait on God and walk with Him.

The above scripture talks about mounting up with wings as eagles, running and not being weary, walking and not fainting. The eagle has the longest lifespan of the bird species. It can live up to 70 years, but to reach this age, the eagle must make a hard decision in its 40s. The long and flexible talons can no longer grab the prey which serves as food. Its long and sharp beak becomes bent. Its old-aged and heavy wings, due to their thick feathers, become stuck to its chest and make it difficult to fly. Then the eagle is left with only two options; die, or go through a painful process of change, which lasts about 150 days. The process requires the eagle to fly to the mountain top and sit on its nest. The eagle then knocks its beak against a rock until it falls out. After this, the eagle will wait for a new beak to grow; then it will pluck out its talons.

When its new talons grow back, the eagle starts plucking its old-aged feathers. After about five months, the eagle takes its famous flight of rebirth and lives for 30 more years. When an old eagle is going through the renewal process, other eagles come and provide food for it until new feathers grow again and it changes to a new eagle and is renewed. The other eagles continue to support the old eagle. Just like the old eagle positioning itself in the sun and waiting for its feathers to drop off so that it can be renewed, we need to position ourselves before our Lord to go through a renewal process.

Over the years, after giving our lives to the Lord Jesus, for us to walk and not faint, we need to, on a daily basis, wait on the Lord to get rid of the bad character we have attracted in our souls. Our souls have layers that stored up information or images, whether good or bad. Our souls get contaminated through persons, locations and things we come in contact with. For example, for a person that has gone through abuse, that trauma or pain is registered in their soul. Waiting on the Lord enables our Lord Jesus to go right into those layers and touch and get rid of the pain and trauma permanently. After which, rebirth takes place, and we can do exploits again. In the place of waiting, the Holy Spirit brings to the attention the persons, places, things that tie to our souls, release them, retrieve our parts (self) deposited to them, and we release them from our souls. Without this process, we cannot operate effectively in the things of God.

At this stage, we are renewed, like the eagle, and insight is imparted to us. During the process, talents, strengths, etc. are exchanged, the old is removed, and we become new creatures. We receive a new touch from the Lord, which causes us to be translated from darkness to the kingdom of light, and we see clearly. When this process is taking place, prayer becomes easy and answers come speedily.

As I said earlier, the early church waited on God, and we have lost a great heritage (present church) for not being able to come before our Father, talk with Him face to face, wait until he (in heaven) answers us. Matthew 7:7: 'Seek and you shall find.' This is not about naming and claiming, for God hates laziness.

What is waiting on God?

Waiting on God can be defined as follows:

1. Standing still before God. Psalm 46:10: 'Be still and know that he is God...'
2. Being quiet in his presence. You have spoken to Him; now it is his turn to speak back to you. Psalm 62:1: 'Truly my soul waited upon God...'
3. Just as the waters under heaven gather together in one place (Genesis 1:9) wait until our souls gather together in oneness with Him.
4. Coming to God with a loving expectation in his presence. Psalm 130:6: 'My soul waited for the Lord more than they that watch for the morning...' We need to wait earnestly or stay in his presence until we are bonded in intimacy with our Lord.

5. John 15:5&7 says, 'I am the vine, and I in you...'
    'If ye abide in me, and my words abide in you...'
    This simply means, we abide in Him and his
    words abide in us; abiding until we are bound in
    oneness in Him.

6. 1Corrinthians 6:17: 'But he that is joined unto
    the Lord is one spirit.' When we wait in his
    presence, we are joined together in one spirit with
    our Lord Jesus.

7. As stated in Luke 17:21, the kingdom of God is
    within you. Because of this, when transformation
    takes place in your life, you no longer live without
    His direction.

    Psalm 62:5: 'My soul, wait thou only upon God;
    for my expectation is from Him.' Here, your soul
    is silent before the Lord; no movement, no noise.
    Keep silent before the Lord (voices in your head
    must be quieted or muffled — brought under
    control with the help of the Holy Spirit).

God is calling us to come to a place of a closer fellowship
with Him. However, the flesh does hinder us from
coming to God, and talking to Him. When we, as
believers, develop the habit of waiting on the Lord, it
helps us develop intimacy with Him; and as is common
with other relationships, He begins to share things with
us. This could be information, direction and guidance,
divine instructions that if we obey, will do us the world
of good, and avert some ugly experiences. The book of
Amos 3: 7 records, 'Surely the Lord GOD will do
nothing, but he revealeth his secrets to his servants the
Prophets'. Similarly, Deuteronomy 29:29 (NLT) says,

'The LORD our God has secrets known to no one. We are not accountable for them, but we and our children are accountable forever for all that he has revealed to us, so that we may obey all the terms of these instructions.' Yes! As we draw closer to God through waiting on Him and developing intimacy with Him, he will no doubt begin to reveal some of these secret things to us for our own betterment. That is walking with the LORD. Again, Amos 3:3 says, 'Can two walk together unless they are agreed?' How can we even come to an agreement if we do not hear Him? All these emphasise the importance of waiting on the Lord as an ingredient for walking with Him. This is also an indication that Enoch and Noah, whom the Bible records as having walked with the Lord, must have waited or had quiet times with their God. In that place intimacy, He will also show us his kingdom. We must remember that, as believers in Jesus Christ, we are first called to minister to God, then people. As waiters in a restaurant wait for us to place our orders, so it is with us: we wait on God and take orders from Him before we minister to each other.

THE ESSENCE OF WAITING ON GOD OR HAVING QUIET TIME WITH HIM

When we wait on the Lord, we receive the character transformation of humility.

Proverbs 6:18 says, 'the Lord hates a proud look', and 1Peter 5:5-6 says, 'Likewise, ye younger, submit yourself onto the elder, yea, all of you be subject one to another, and be clothed with humility, for God resisteth the proud, and giveth grace to the humble. Humble yourselves therefore under the mighty hand of God that he may exalt you in due time.'

Satan is an expert in legalism and uses the law (the great commandments) to accuse us before God. The devil can detect our sins simply by observing what we believers are doing to each other. Satan is the mastermind of all evil. He will entice us with his lies and all manner of evil to formulate his plans and lead us to foster rebellion against the Lord. When we, as believers, fall into his trap, he steals that which God has deposited in us for his (Satan's) trophy room.

A book called *Heaven Awaits the Bride,* written by Anna Rountree, gives us an account of what she saw when she was taken to Satan's trophy room by the Lord Jesus. She said that in this room, she saw on display the just measure, Miriam's tambourine, Bezalel's renderings for the workers (of the patterns given to Moses on the mount), and the widow's bowl had various musical instruments of ancient design. According to her, these could have been taken into the enemy's camp because of the sins of God's people.

The visit to Satan's trophy room was to recover the embroidered robe; the garment that was lost through disobedience to the Lord in his church. The garment reflected the heart of compassion, kindness, humility, gentleness, and patience. Also bearing with one another, and forgiving each other. Thank God, with the help of our Lord, Anna Rountree was able to recover the robe. When we put on the garment of humility, with all its attributes, we can enter into a deeper relationship with Jesus Christ, as well as a deeper covenant with his body.

The second thing that happens to us is the *earnest desire* to dwell in the house of the Lord all our lives, to behold his glory and always inquire as to what to do (Psalm 27:4). Man was not created to be alone. We were created to have fellowship with our maker — our God. Psalm 84:2: 'My soul longeth, yea even fainteth for the courts of the Lord, my heart, and flesh crieth out for the living God.' God created man and put a yearning in our souls to be filled with love, happiness, joy, and peace. When these are lacking in our lives, instead of seeking God to fill our souls with that fellowship of love and peace in Him, we reach out to things of the world which do not last, or even seek Satan in fellowship to our destruction.

The third phase is the character transformation of consecration. To consecrate means to set someone or something apart as holy unto God for his use (Exodus 19:22-23). God is the one who consecrates (Exodus 29:44). He may also use a man of God to act for Him, as he did with Moses (Exodus 29:1). God may also ask individuals to consecrate themselves for his work.

Exodus 24:16-18 says, 'And the glory of God abode upon mount Sinai, and the cloud covered it six days, and the seventh day he called unto Moses out of the mist of the cloud. And the sight of the glory of the Lord was like a devouring fire on the top of the mount in the eyes of the children of Israel. And Moses went into the mist of the cloud and got him up into the mount, and Moses was in the mount forty days and forty nights.'

2 5

Moses waited under a cloud of glory on the mount for six days for the fire of God to purify his spirit, soul, and body, after which he was qualified to enter God's glory for forty days and forty nights. As an eagle waits before the sun to transform, so do we. We have to wait for the fire of purification to transform us to meet with the Lord.

Fourthly, the transformation of the Holy Spirit enables us to get into the secret place of God. Exodus 33:21: 'And the Lord said, behold, there is a place by me, and thou shall stand upon a rock.' Jesus Christ had paid the full price to gain access to the Father, the blood of Jesus Christ, as well as the anointing oil sprinkled upon us, which qualified us to enter that secret place of God. We need to shut the doors of our minds and hearts and gather in oneness with God. Waiting in the place by Him requires us to pay the price, which is surrendering our time to Him.

Mathew 14:23 says, 'And when he had sent the multitudes away, he went up into the mountain apart to pray, and when the evening came, he was there alone.' Just as Jesus Christ did, we need to set a time of day to meet with the Lord.

Chapter three

ENCOUNTER WITH THE LORD

Psalm 46:10 declares, 'Be still, and know that I am God; I will be exalted among the heathens, I will be exalted in the earth.' For us to have an encounter with the Lord, we need to be still before Him. Our minds, emotions, thoughts, imaginations — everything needs to be shut out, and we just keep silence before Him. Anxiety or worrying thoughts will not help us. God wants us, as his children, to know about his house or kingdom. John 14:1-2 says, 'Let not your heart be troubled: ye believe in God, also believe in me, in my Father's house are many mansions; if it were not so, I would have told you. I go to prepare a place for you.'

In God's kingdom, there are planes of existence. For instance, each angelic being or group has its level (home/house), and there are different levels for the saints and other beings that we are not aware of. Entering into the throne of God, the cloak of humility is required. A proud person cannot walk with God. Most of the so-called celebrities in our days feel they don't need God. More often, we hear people say things such as, 'I don't do God.'

Psalm 39:5 says, 'Behold, thou hast made my days as an handbreadth, and my age is as nothing before thee: verily every man at his best state is altogether vanity.' Our breath, times are all in his hands. God determines everything about us — we must be humble before Him, all the time. The Bible tells us that Moses was the meekest of men on the face of the earth (Numbers 12:3). Because of Moses's humility, the Lord will speak to him face to face. History also records that Saint Francis Assisi walked with God with humility of heart. He was born to very wealthy parents but became homeless to take care of the poor. He had several encounters with the Lord and always waited in his presence for direction. Mother Theresa is another saint that walked with God with humility of heart. She also had a deep relationship with the Lord Jesus.

There are physical and spiritual benefits to waiting on the Lord. When we wait on the Lord, the following takes place in our physical bodies, for it is written that the body is the temple of God (1Corrinthians 6:19). To fully understand why our bodies are called temples of God, we need to look at the pattern of the heavenly tabernacle shown to Moses by God. The tabernacle is our roadmap to enter his presence.

Step I: The gate

Jesus Christ, the Son of the living God, is the gate. When we come to the gate, we see our Lord Jesus. This is a born-again experience. (New life experience in the Lord Jesus). At this point, we must see Jesus as a saviour in our lives and the King of glory (our King).

Step II: His court (dealing with our flesh)

The courts are between the gates and the altar. As we come into court with praise and worship to God, our strength is being renewed. The eagle's strength is renewed as it positions itself in the sun. Our strength is renewed as we look at the cross of Jesus (brazen altar in the tabernacle). True worship starts at the cross, which is also the altar of sacrifice, where Jesus's blood was shed. In the Old Testament the tabernacle (courtyard) has four horns, which represent the following in the New Testament:

- Forgiveness of our sins (Romans 3:25)
- Deliverance from every bondage (2 Corinthians 5:21). We are now made righteous through His blood sacrifice at the cross.
- Old man crucified — our old nature is dead (Romans 6:6)
- Our bodies become living sacrifices, and we are also transformed by the renewing of our minds. (Romans 12:1-2). A change occurs as the filthiness in our souls is removed. We depend on the blood of Jesus to cleanse us. We take hold of the altar (cross of Jesus) and ask forgiveness of our sins. As we move to the next level at courts, there is a level of brass — a place of sanctification through His word, where the work of flesh is dissolved until there are no wrinkles, blemishes, etc. and our bodies become his temple. Psalm 92:10 says, 'But my horn shalt thou exalt like the horn of a unicorn; I shall be anointed with fresh oil.' When we wait on the Lord, we are anointed

with fresh oil; the damaged cells in our bodies are renewed. You see somebody who is 60 years old, looking 40–50 years old. Moses was 120 years old when he died, and his eyes were not dim, and his natural body was not abated. (Deuteronomy 34:7).

The Bible says, 'The spirit of man is the candle of the Lord, searching all the inwards parts of the belly', Proverbs 20:27. Also Matthew 5:14 says, 'ye are the light of the world...' As the light of God increases in us while we wait in his presence, there is a process taking place in us and we are full of the Lord, thereby laziness is removed, and a brand new strength is imparted in us.

Step III: Holy place (place of service – ministry work)

You will run and not be weary. Most of us Christians get stuck in the courtyard and would not go further. Many of us become frustrated, dry, and weary in our walk with God. The holy place is where our soul is being dealt with by the Holy Spirit, which is dealing with will and mind. In this holy place, we see the candlesticks/lampstand (menorah) with seven branches, which stands on its own. Isaiah 11:2 says, 'And the spirit of the Lord shall rest upon Him, the spirit of wisdom and understanding the spirit of counsel and might, the spirit of knowledge and the fear of the Lord.' When the spirit of the Lord rests upon us, while waiting in the presence, we receive wisdom and understanding (illumination — insight on what to do). We receive spiritual counsel from the Holy Spirit and the spirit of might to do the work assigned to us. The spirit of knowledge — making the word of God easy to understand — and the Holy Spirit imparts the spirit of the fear of God, as we read the Bible.

At the lampstand, the Holy Spirit deals with our mind/intellect. It is a place where our mind is renewed. 2Corinthians 10:5: 'Casting down imaginations, and every high thing that exalteth itself against the knowledge of God, and bringing into captivity every thought to the obedience of Christ.' Underneath the lampstand is oil (a type of Holy Spirit) and wicks for lighting. These wicks need constant cleaning to remove all the pollution from our minds. This enables illumination by the Holy Spirit (oil) from the lamp sticks to shine. His mind becomes our mind. (Philippians 2:5.)

Then the Shaw bread or table of bread (symbol of the word of God). It also signifies the logos — the written word of God. The table of bread deals with our will. Waiting in his presence, here the Holy Spirit translates the Logos to Rhema word. In other words, the Holy Spirit makes His word available to our specific needs. This is where praying and groaning in the spirit takes place in our prayers. His word begins to work in us with power. The word of God becomes our prayer.

There is coming the move of God (which has started manifestation), where true worship and his word would be coming out of our being with power. This is where true intercession takes place. One is no longer concerned with their own needs, but with his needs. This is the time when success is not how big your church is, but doing the will of God. On the table of bread, there is a pure incense. When the pure incence is being sprinkled, the fragrance from the incense is released at the table of bread. What takes place here is that our will is exchanged to his will, and we surrender all. Hebrews 10:5-7, Jesus surrendered his will to God. When our will in exchange for his own will here, it becomes easy for his own will here; it becomes easy for us to surrender our minds at the lampstand.

Step IV Holy of Holies

This is a place where strength is imparted to you by God the Father Himself, where you can walk and not faint. The ark of covenant becomes a reality in your life, Christ in you; the hope of glory. Hebrews 9:1-8: "Then verily the first covenant had also ordinances of divine services, and a worldly sanctuary. For there was a tabernacle made; the first, containing the candlestick and the table, and the showbread: which is called the sanctuary. And after the second veil; the tabernacle, which is called the Holiest of all. This had the golden censer, and the ark of the covenant overlaid with gold, wherein was the golden pot that had manna and Aaron's rod that budded, and the tables of the covenant. And over it the cherubim of glory shadowing the mercy seat of which we cannot now speak particularly. Now when these things were thus ordained, the priests went always into the first tabernacle, accomplishing the service of God.

But into the second went the priest alone once every year, not without blood, which he offered for Himself, for the errors of the people. The Holy Ghost thus signified that the way into the Holiest of all was not yet made manifest, while the first tabernacle was yet standing." (For further reading of the pattern of the earthly tabernacle shown to Moses on the mount read Exodus 25.)

Jesus Christ is our high priest and offered Himself once for all our sins and anything that was written against us. Now we come boldly to the throne of grace to obtain mercy for our past, present and future sins. The price has been paid through the blood of Jesus. In the Holy of Holies, only one person is allowed to enter. This is our meeting with God Almighty Himself, and there is no natural light needed; only the light of God, permeating through the mercy seat.

The incenses on the altar (four in number) are being released, and there is smoke all over the place (signifying the glory of God covering the Holiest of all). God is a spirit, and we must worship Him in spirit and truth (John 4:24). This we must do when we enter into his presence. We join God in one spirit, having true intimacy with Him, becoming one with our Lord Jesus in worship. When this takes place, there is an unlocking of our emotions as the incense runs through the veil, causing one to loosen up in his presence.

As the incense is rising, our spirit man is released to enter his presence and is completely lost in him. We are broken before him as all bondages, limitation, fear, slavery and all filthiness are removed. Psalm 46:10 becomes our experience as we sit still in silence and wait. Our words become few and our Lord Jesus takes over and does all the talking. In other words, our tongues are loosening, but they are no longer ours, but his. As we go deep into intimacy with our Lord Jesus, deep worship begins to come from our inner beings, worshipping and celebrating the blood of Jesus on the mercy seat. John 17:24: '...that they may behold my glory...' This is a place where we behold his Shekinah glory. We disappear, and Jesus takes over. It is important to note the blood that never disappears as God the Father looks on the mercy seat and He sees the blood of his Son Jesus Christ. The cherubims covering the mercy seat see the blood and also protect the glory of God.

Hebrews 9:4-5: 'Which had the golden censer, and the ark of the covenant overlaid round about with gold, wherein was the golden pot that had Manna, and Aaron's rod that budded, and the tables of the covenant. And over it the cherubims of glory shadowing the mercy seat; of which we cannot now speak particularly.' The scripture speaks about the manna, which is the bread of life (the word) and Jesus is the bread of life and the living word, and Aaron's rod, signifying his power.

In 2 Chronicles 5:7-10, when the ark of the covenant was brought forth, there was nothing in the ark, save the two tables of stone which Moses put therein in Horeb (the law only was in the ark). 1Corinthians 9:20-21 says, 'And unto the Jews I became as a Jew, that I might gain the Jews; to them that are under the law, as under the law, that I might gain them that are under the law. To them that are without law, as without law, (being not without the law of God but under the law of Christ) that it might gain them that are without law.'

The law is hidden in Christ Jesus, which is the significance of putting only the law in the ark of the covenant. We worship the Father for the blood of Jesus that not only gives access to his presence but has redeemed us and paid all our past, present, and future sins. We are made righteous through his blood, and we have become righteous through Jesus Christ, our Lord and saviour.

We see the devil (the accuser) and his co-hosts stripped, disarmed and defeated, therefore no more fear, shame, slavery, bondage, failure and so on. We are free from fear of Satan, intimidations, and the breaking of God's commandments not through our hard work in keeping them. We see the grace of God working in us, for it is only because of his grace that we are what we are today. In this place, called the Holy of Holies, while waiting in his presence, we develop a deep relationship with the Lord. We go through a moulding experience. The Lord feeds us with spiritual food to strengthen us and impart us with his grace, and the authority to wage war against Satan and his hosts.

We are now rising up with wings, like an eagle, to fly again. This practice of waiting on the Lord does not take place overnight; the Holy Spirit helps us to go through the process until we are mature enough to translate in the realm of the supernatural. The Bible records the following people as those who have experienced translation of the soul, spirit, or body.

Moses went up into the mountain, and cloud covered the whole mountain. The glory of the Lord abode upon

Mount Sinai and the clouds covered it for six days. On the seventh day, the Lord spoke to Moses (Exodus 24:15-16). Moses was transported to heaven and given the pattern of the tabernacle. Hebrews 8:5 says, 'Who serve unto the example and shadow of heavenly things, as Moses was admonished of God when he was about to make the tabernacle; for see, saith he, that thou make all things according to the pattern shown to thee in the mount.'

Ezekiel 3:12-14: 'The spirit of the Lord took him up, and behind him, he heard a voice of a great rushing saying, Blessed be the glory of the LORD from his place. I heard also the noise of the wings of the living creatures that touched one another, and the noise of the wheels over against them, and a noise of a great rushing.' Ezekiel spoke of the spirit lifting him and taking him away, and the hand of the Lord was strong upon him.

Apostle John, the writer of the Book of Revelation, records a series of visions God gave him about Jesus Christ; not about Jesus' earthly ministry, but about the continuing work of Jesus from heaven, using the gospel and the church. John saw a magnificent vision of Jesus standing among his churches (Revelation 1:12-20). He saw a vision of God's throne (Revelation 4) and Jesus as a lamb (Revelation 5), then John described his visions of the lamb opening the seven seals of a scroll (chapters 6, 7 and 8). In the last chapter, he described his visions of the ultimate destruction of evil and the emergence of God's holy city from heaven.

Apostle Paul's vision of the Lord talks about his visions and revelations. He said he (Paul) was caught up to the third heaven and was also caught up into paradise and heard unspeakable words which no man can utter (2Corrinthians 12:1-4).

How do we translate?

Our God may use many ways for us to transport from earth to his heavenly kingdom. However, the few that come to mind from Bible recordings are as follows:

a) We are informed, in Genesis 28:11-12, that when Jacob came to a certain place (known as Jacob's dream at Bethel) and tarried there all night, he took stones for his pillows and lay down to sleep. He dreamed and beheld a ladder set up on the earth, and the top of it reached to heaven, and beheld the angels of God ascending and descending it.

In the 1980s, I had an experience that shocked me for life. I found myself before the Lord Jesus, and joined the heavenly beings to worship Him. I remember this particular angel who turned around to look at me as we all bowed down to worship the Lord Jesus. This angel had blue eyes and was sparkling with lights. His appearance scared me a bit, however, because I was in the presence of the Lord Jesus, I just ignored this angel and continued with my worship of the Lord. After the worship, the Lord gave me a message to the church concerning our worship to

God the Father, Son (Jesus) and the Holy Spirit. He later told me to go back to the earth, and I started descending from a very long ladder made of pure light. Although the ladder was long, from heaven to earth, the journey was very short.

b) An Angel will come to take you. In Revelation 17:1-3: 'And there came one of the seven angels which had the seven vials, and talked with me, saying unto me, come hither; I will show unto thee the judgement of the great whore that sitteth upon many waters. With whom the kings of the earth have committed fornication, and the inhabitants of the earth have been made drunk with the wine of her fornication. So he carried me away in the spirit into the wilderness; and I saw a woman sit upon a scarlet coloured beast, full of names of blasphemy, having seven heads and ten horns.'

As the close of the age is drawing nearer, angelic escorts to the spiritual world are increasing. Many saints are being taken by these angels to show us the mystery of this other world (the spirit realm) which is more real than our earthly world.

c) Elijah was taken away to heaven by a chariot of fire. 2Kings 2:11: 'And it came to pass, as they still went on, and talked, that behold, there appeared a chariot of fire, and horses of fire, parted them both asunder, and Elijah went up by a whirlwind into heaven.'

d) The Holy Spirit took Philip away after ministering salvation and baptizing an Ethiopian eunuch in the desert. The eunuch came to Jerusalem to worship and was returning to Ethiopia. He was in his chariot reading the book of Isaiah, but could not understand. The Holy Spirit told Philip to go near and explain what (Isaiah 53:7) was talking about, which was the fulfilment of prophecy about the Lord Jesus's death on the cross to save us. Acts 8:38-39 say, 'And He commanded the chariot to stand still: And they went down both in the water, both Philip, and the eunuch; and he baptized him. And when they were come up out of the water, the Spirit of the Lord caught away Philip, that the eunuch saw him no more; and he went on his way rejoicing.'

e) Jesus Christ Himself may appear to us, choose us, equip us for ministry, work and anoint us into our specific calling. Psalm 65:4: 'Blessed is the man whom thou choosest and causest to approach unto thee, that he may dwell in thy courts, we shall be satisfied with the goodness of thy house, even of thy house, even of thy holy temple.' Apart from men and women of God, ordinary men, women, young and old, more than ever before, are seeing Jesus appearing to them in dreams. I read a story of a woman recently who was sick and dreamed that Jesus gave her water to drink and when she got up in the morning, she was healed. She also saw a written note on her bedside table her saying Jesus is the living and true God. Ever since this happened, she has been talking about Jesus, and many are giving their lives to Him. We find testimonies of former atheists, Buddhists, Muslims, etc. claiming they had died, had afterlife experiences, but were saved and brought back by Jesus Christ.

The Lord Jesus said, 'I am with you always even unto the end of the world.' (Mathew 28: 20.) The Lord has not left us stranded; he is always with us. I had seen Him many times when we gathered together in his name to worship Him. Mantels are being released these days not only for ministry work but also in the marketplace.

f) Our worship of the Lord helps to enhance the translation experience. Psalm 84:4 says, 'Blessed are they that dwell in thy house, they will be still praising thee.' And also in Psalm 22:3, 'But thou art holy, o thou that inhabitest the praise of Israel.' When we praise and worship Him by lifting up our hands to Him, our whole being is in union with the Lord, thus causing the Lord Himself to come and inhabit with us. In 2Chronicles 5:13 and 14, the Bible records that as the trumpeters and singers were as one to make one sound to be heard in praising and thanking the Lord and saying, for he is good; for his mercy endureth forever, then the house of the Lord was filled with a cloud. Priests could not stand to minister because of the cloud, for the glory of the Lord had filled the house of God. This is what our Lord Jesus called true worship; that is worshipping in spirit and truth (John 4). The cloud of glory enhances our worship to be purified by fire, thereby allowing us access to the Holy of Holies.

In December 2002, I attended a world conference by Dr Morris Cerullo in Florida for the first time. As we gathered in the large hall for the morning session, we were all lost in intense worship, when suddenly, in an open vision, I saw a ladder appear. Heaven opened above us. It was as though there was no roof over us, as I could see the angels descending and ascending. I also saw Jesus come in, and thousands and thousands of angels joined us in worshipping the Lord. Many lives were touched that day; healings, miracles, and breakthroughs. That was the turning point in my spiritual walk with the Lord. From that day on, I longed to be in his presence all the time. Something within me that I cannot explain. In closing, however, I want to send a warning to everyone reading this: don't build your life on spiritual experience, but first ground yourself in the word of God (the Bible). Don't run from the experience but let the word of God be in you so that your life is balanced with the Lord. The devil also translates (Mathew 4:5-8), in Mathew 4:5: 'The devil taketh Him up into the holy city and setteth Him on a pinnacle of the temple.'

Chapter four

Pray and wait on the Lord every day

Many of us rush in and out of prayer without allowing Him (the Lord) to speak back to us and reveal his plan to us. Everything around us is quick, with no time to wait. "God I have spoken to you, thank you for listening, and I will talk to you later, bye and love you always." Even when the Holy Spirit is trying to draw our minds to relax and listen, we are not prepared to do so. No wonder our walk with God has become boring.

God is speaking to us every day, and he loves to do this all the time. He has given us the power to pull our minds back and make them still. In our human nature, while we are in prayer and also waiting before the Lord to show us things we do not know, believe me, that is the time that our mind begins to wander here and there. However, we have the power to command our mind to align with the mind of our Lord Jesus. Rebuke every negative voice, image, imagination in the name of Jesus and bring the blood of Jesus against every hindrance; command these forces to bow by the blood of Jesus in Jesus's name. Do this as often as possible until the door is open. Master the art of waiting on the Lord. It is possible to live in the two worlds at the same time (spiritual and physical), but we need to be still.

2Kings 5:25-26: 'But he went in, and stood before his master. And Elisha said unto him, whence comest thou, Gehazi? And he said, thy servant went no whither. And he said unto him, went not my heart with thee when the man turned again from his chariot to meet thee? Is it a time to receive money, and to receive garments and love yards and vineyards and sheep, and oxen, and menservants and maidservants?' After Naaman was healed of leprosy, he wanted to give the prophet Elisha changes of raiment, silver, gold and other gifts to express his gratitude. Elisha, however, refused the gifts, but his servant Gehazi ran after Naaman and lied to him, saying, "after you left, two young prophets came, and although my master wouldn't take anything for himself, he said it was all right to take some changes of raiment and some talents of silver and gold for these prophets." Naaman was so happy to be healed that he gave Gehazi twice as much as he asked for. Then Gehazi hid the gifts and stood before his master, Elisha. When he returned, and Elisha asked him where he had been, he said: "Nowhere, my master." Elisha said, "My heart (spirit) went with you when you caught up with that chariot, I saw you." How could Elisha, sitting in his own house, know what was going on, several miles away? God revealed it to him; God gave Elisha supernatural revelation of what had happened. To me, this is an example of living in both the spiritual and physical realm at the same time.

In Genesis 1:27, the Bible records that we are created in the image of God. God did not create us to live here on earth not knowing who we are and why we are here. God made us in his image to know Him and obey his word, leading us into his plan and purpose. When we read God's word and meditate on his word, we abide in Him, and his words abide in us, and as we ask whatever we want, it is done unto us (John 15:7). Feeding on the word of God, our spirit man is quickened, for the word of God is life-giving for his words are spiritual food (John 6:63). In other words, the breadth of the Lord is released unto us as we feast on his words.

Mathew 4:4 "But he answered and said, it is written, man shall not live by bread alone but by every word that proceedeth out of the mouth of God." We need the spirit of God to understand his word. It is important to note here that we read his words first, meditate on his words, pray and wait patiently before the Lord. Why the word of God? Because we need to speak back his words to Him to receive.

For instance, I remember when I was in Nigeria, I travelled to Makurdi for a conference. I left my children (five years old) for two weeks in Kaduna (which is over 500 kilometres from Makurdi) and was missing them. I spoke to my Heavenly Father concerning their welfare when suddenly the presence of the Lord became so strong in the room and before my very eyes, I saw an angel standing there with my two boys, sound and healthy. In a flash, the angel and my children vanished. Immediately, the burden was lifted, and I started praising God. After a few days, I travelled back to Kaduna and found Joshua and Caleb sound and well.

Proverbs 18:4 says, 'The words of a man's mouth are as deep waters, and the well spring of wisdom as a flowing brook.'

When a man is thirsty, and he takes water in his mouth, he receives freshness, purification and life-giving. The word of God is like water in our mouths.

Proverbs 20:5: 'Counsel in the heart of man is like deep water; but a man of understanding will draw it out.'

Waiting and meditating on the word of God enables us, with the help of the Holy Spirit to go deep within us, like a deep well. With a full focus in our mind, the word of God enables us to draw from the fountain which is the heart of our Lord Jesus. There are four levels of increasing revelation as we continue to meditate on his words.

Ezekiel 47:3-7 says, 'And when the man that had the line in his hand went forth eastward, he measured a thousand cubits, and he brought me through the waters, the waters were to the ankles. And again he measured a thousand and brought me through the waters; the waters were to the knees. Again he measured a thousand and brought me through the water to the loins. Afterwards, he measured a thousand, and it was a river that I could not pass over, for the waters were risen, waters to swim in a river that could not be passed over. And he said unto me, son of man, has thou seen this? Then he brought me, and caused me to return to the bank of the river. Now when I had returned, behold at the bank of the river were very many trees on the one side and the other.'

The ankle level represents our basic level of revelation. Job says, there is a spirit in man, and the inspiration of the Almighty giveth them understanding. Job 32:8.

The knee level is where we hear the Holy Spirit teach us. The Holy Spirit anoints us and dwells within us, teaching us all things which no man can teach us. He is the Spirit of truth that cannot lie. He is our teacher who teaches us all the time (1John 2:27).

Jesus is speaking in John 16:13: 'Howbeit when he, the Spirit of truth comes, he will guide you into all truth; for he shall not speak of Himself; but whatsoever he shall hear, that he shall speak and he will show you things to come.'

I depend on the Holy Spirit at all times to give me a revelation, even as I write this book.

The waist level experience is where the angelic being comes to teach us. Daniel had a vision and sought the meaning. He saw a man stand before him. He also heard the voice of a man telling Gabriel (an archangel) to make Daniel understand the vision (Daniel 8:15-16).

Also in Revelation 1:1: 'The revelation of Jesus Christ, which God gave unto Him to show unto his servant's things which must shortly come to pass; and he sent and signified it by his angel unto his servant John.'

In addition to the angelic beings sent by God to teach us, the saints of God who have gone to be with the Lord may come to give revelation from the Lord.

We see this in Luke 9:28-31: 'And it came to pass about an eight days after these sayings, he took Peter and John and James and went up into a mountain to pray. And as he prayed, the fashion of his countenance was altered, and his raiment was white and glistering. And behold, there talked with Him two men who were Moses and Elias; who appeared in glory and spoke of his decease which he should accomplish at Jerusalem.'

Before Jesus Christ went to the cross to be crucified, Moses and Elijah came to talk to Him about it. As we are coming close to rapture, heaven and earth must come closer.

The final level, which is also the fourth level experience, is known as the neck level, where Jesus Christ, our Lord and saviour, teaches us his word. The Lord Himself enlightened our eyes (Psalm 119:8); illuminating our eyes, both natural and spiritual, to discover both realms, turning his visitation to his habitation. The Lord, Jesus Himself, gave us eyes of understanding in our hearts (Ephesians 1:18) to know the riches of his glory. Our eyes are always open, like those of an eagle.

In 2Kings 6:16-17, Elisha saw in both realms, physical and spiritual. When the servant of Elisha saw that their home was encompassed by a host army with horses and chariots, he cried out to the man of God. Elisha told him not to fear for he (Elisha) had seen that the host of heaven (warring angels) were more with them than the physical army. Elisha prayed for the servant's eyes to open and the Lord opened the eyes of the servant, and he saw that the mountain (their dwelling) was full of horses and chariots of fire about Elisha.

It is interesting to know that we, as human beings, do not have the desire to seek God Almighty; however, the

Lord Himself put the desire in us to hunger and thirst for Him. No wonder David says, 'As the hart panteth after the water brooks, so panteth my soul after thee, O God. My soul thirsteth for God, for the living God, when shall I come and appear before God?' (Psalm 42:1-2)

The Lord Jesus knows his own and is always drawing us to run after Him. We can create habitation where God will come and dwell in and angelic appearance, becoming a common phenomenon. This takes place in our prayer closet where we meet God, one to one.

In Exodus 25:8-9, God told Moses to make Him a sanctuary that he may dwell among them. Accordingly, God showed Moses the pattern of the tabernacle to make it. In this tabernacle, there is the outer court, the Holy place, and the Holy of Holies.

The outer is what we can call the first realm of prayer, which represents the asking realm. In this realm, we come with our dull and troubled minds harassed by the devil. This is a realm where we are battling with our flesh, hearing voices of devils and rebuking them in Jesus's name. Very little victories are achieved here, and sadly many rush in and out, thinking they have accomplished their prayer tasks, and answers are on the way. This realm is also a place where we spend much time repenting and repenting, again and again, each time we come into the prayer closet. It is sad to note that here in the outer court, God is not near, and that is why it is called the outer court.

The next realm is seeking fellowship or, better still, the waiting level. It is a realm where we take the time to pursue and have fellowship with the Holy Spirit. In this realm, I will pray quietly in the language of the Holy Spirit and wait for his leading. In this realm, which is known as the Holy place, the Holy Spirit is in control, and he begins to pray through us to enter into the third realm. In the second realm, the Holy Spirit prepares us to thirst for the living God, where we are ready to appear before Him (Psalm 42:2). It is very important to know that in the first realm, the blood of Jesus cleanses us from dead works or sins, which also prepares us to enter the Holy place.

In Hebrew 9:1-16: 'Then verily the first covenant had also ordinances of divine service and a worldly sanctuary. For there was a tabernacle made; the first, wherein was the candlestick and the table and the showbread; which is called the sanctuary. And after second veil the tabernacle, which is called the Holiest of all; which had the golden censer and the ark of the covenant overlaid round about with gold, where in was the golden pot that had manna, and Aaron's rod that budded, and the tables of the covenant. And over it the cherubims of glory shadowing the mercy seat; of which we cannot now speak particularly. Now when these things were thus ordained, the priests went always into the first tabernacle, accomplishing the service of God. But into the second went the high priest alone once every year, not without blood which he offered for himself and the errors of the people.

The Holy Ghost this signifying, that the way into the Holiest of all was not yet made manifest, while as the first tabernacle was yet standing, which was a figure for the time then present, in which were offered both gifts and sacrifices, that could not make him that did the service perfect as pertaining to the conscience. Which stood only in meats and drinks, and divers washings, and carnal ordinances imposed on them until the time of reformation. But Christ being come an high priest of good things to come, by a greater and more perfect tabernacle, not made with hands that is to say, not of this building, Neither by the blood of goats and calves, but by his own blood he entered in once into the holy place, having obtained eternal redemption for us. For if the blood of bulls and goats and the ashes of an heifer sprinkling the unclean, sanctifieth to the purifying of the flesh. How much more shall the blood of Christ, who through the eternal Spirit offered Himself without spot to God, purge your conscience from dead works to serve the living God? And for this cause, he is the mediator of the New Testament, that by means of death, for the redemption of the transgression that were under the first testament, they which are called might receive the promise of eternal inheritance. For where a testament is there must also of necessity be the death of the testator.'

The scripture in Hebrew 9:1 described how the pattern of the earthly tabernacle was made, which also was to us the shadow of the heavenly pattern. Jesus Christ, our high priest, died on the cross two thousand years ago, just as the earthly high priest entered the Holy of Holies every year to offer sacrifice using the blood of bulls and goats for himself and the nation of Israel, Jesus Christ did the same. Jesus Christ entered into the Holy of

Holies as the high priest only once, not yearly, with his blood in the heavenly tabernacle. With his blood, he appeared in the presence of God for us. With his blood, he purified the mercy seat, things in heaven, sacrificed Himself for us, blotting out all our past, present and future sins, failures, curses, bondages, slavery, etc. He reconciled us to God and opened heaven for us. His blood purged the law that Satan uses to accuse us. We are free from Satan and his demons. We are now the righteousness of God through Jesus Christ our Lord and high priest.

As mentioned earlier, in the second realm (holy place), the place of seeking and fellowshipping with the Holy Spirit, he (the Holy Spirit) quickens our soul, prepares us to meet with our high priest, the Lord Himself. Jesus now leads us to the Holy of Holies.

The Holy of Holies is a place of knocking, a place of intimacy, of one to one in his presence. Psalm 91 becomes a reality as we dwell in his secret place and abide under his shadow. It is a secret place that Satan and demons cannot enter. This realm is a place of glory and peace as one's emotions loosen. This realm is where wisdom originates, and it is a place of understanding who our God is — love. It is a place hidden from the eyes of all living vultures, evil spirits or demons. Destruction and death are kept away, and God alone understands the way (Job 28:20-23).

In this place, God removes obstacles, overthrows mountains, breaks gates into pieces and cuts iron bars asunder. All barriers are broken; he stops the flood and evil rivers from coming near us. He dries them up completely. The evil beasts cannot see us, nor touch us. His plans and purpose become our plans and purpose for the rest of our lives. We are no longer distracted as we remain focused on Him alone.

In Exodus 30:23-32, the Lord gave Moses specification on the types of spices (four in number) mixed with oil of olive to make a holy oil. Each of the spices has a significant meaning. The oil of olive is to be used to anoint the tabernacle of the congregation, of their testimony, the table and his vessels and altar of incense. The altar of burnt offerings, and all his vessels, and the laver and his foot. These were sanctified, and they became holy. Aaron and his sons were also anointed, consecrated that they may minister unto the Lord in the priest's office.

As we proceed further to enter into this third realm in our prayer, Jesus, our anointed high priest, releases his fragrance; the four special spices mingling with the olive oil begins to flow on us. We begin to come into union with our God, which produces a mingling of our lives to his. 'I in them, and thou in me, that they may be made perfect in one.' (John 17:23).

This is a realm where the presence of God becomes so powerful in our prayers that our words become few. The Holy Spirit now prays through us, groaning without utterance. The Holy Spirit blows on the spices mingling with oil, causing a release of Jesus Christ's fragrances. Before our very being, we experience his deep love for us, permeating our inner beings. As the depth of the

Lord's heart of love is revealed to us, we want to abide with Him. We bow down and worship Him, not only as the Son of God, but our Saviour and King of kings. We see his heart still bleeding for us sinners, and we are broken. The Lord Himself begins to purge us from all weakness, going deep into the layers of our souls and purging us of things that should not be there (our secret sins, pains, failures, errors etc.). We experience a great transformation in our lives, and his name in our mouths becomes an ointment poured forth; healing and comforting in his name. We begin to work in the realm of signs and wonders.

www.ingramcontent.com/pod-product-compliance
Lightning Source LLC
Chambersburg PA
CBHW021222020426
42331CB00003B/422